NOBODY'S CHILD

SHARON YEE SPENCER

For permission requests, write to the publisher, addressed:
Jacinth Media Productions
Allentown, PA
info@JacinthMediaProductions.com

All Scripture quotes are taken from the Holy Bible, King James Version, Cambridge, 1769; and The ESV® Bible (The Holy Bible, English Standard Version®). ESV® Text Edition: 2016. Copyright © 2001 by Crossway, a publishing ministry of Good News Publishers.

ISBN:
978-1-960594-41-9 (paperback)
978-1-960594-42-6 (Hardback)
978-1-960594-43-3 (Ebook)

This book was printed in the United States.
First Printing
10 9 8 7 6 5 4 3 2 1

Book cover design by Jacinth Media Productions.

CONTENTS

DEDICATION

I dedicate this book to my dear husband, **Wayne**, for bringing out the best in me as my better half, my companion, and my partner in crime. Since day one, you have always been there for me. God purposed us for each other, and He knew exactly what I needed in a husband when He gave me you.

to my four sons, **Andre, Kenton, Leon, and Lucien**—thank you for propelling me into my purpose and for making me a better mother. I am so grateful that I was able to give you the motherly love I never had. You have shown me the true definition of a mother's love. You're God's greatest gifts to me.

To **Alphanso James**, my high school classmate and longtime friend, who inspired me to complete this book. I promised him at our 2019 school reunion that I would publish it, and though years have passed, I'm proud to finally keep that promise.

To **Diana and Michelle Gordon**, whose kindness and initiative opened the door to a life-changing opportunity in the Cayman Islands.

To **Gloria March and family**, whose unwavering support embraced me like a surrogate family. Your kindness, strength, and presence carried me through a chapter that reshaped my life.

And finally, this book is also dedicated to **every motherless child, every abandoned soul, and every person who has ever felt unseen or unloved.**
May these pages remind you that your story matters, your voice has power, and you are not forgotten. You are deeply loved by God, and by the world that still needs your light.

FOREWORD

Neriah LeBlanc

If you're holding this book right now, there's a good chance you're searching for something.

Maybe it's a whisper of hope in a world that feels too loud. Perhaps you're looking for a mirror that shows you the person you used to be, before the world told you to be someone else. Or maybe you just need to know, with every fiber of your being, that you're not alone. That the hurt you carry is valid, the silence you've endured is heard, and the healing you dream of is real.

I know what that search feels like. The path of a survivor is often a solitary one, a maze of shadows where your own echo is your only companion. The world sees a version of you—the person who smiles at the grocery store, the one who shows up for work, the one who seems to have it all together. But you know the truth. You know the history engraved into your soul, the words left unsaid, and the moments when the weight of it all feels unbearable. You know what it feels like to feel voiceless, to feel like your story is a burden, or that it's simply too messy to tell.

You feel the shame of a past you didn't choose and the fear of a future you can't yet imagine.

For too long, the narrative around abuse and trauma has been one of silence and shame. It is said by some that you should carry your pain like a secret, a heavy cloak you can never take off. You're led to believe that your worth is tied to how well you can hide your scars, how quickly you can "get over it," and how flawlessly you can perform in a world that doesn't understand your struggle.

But what if that narrative is wrong? What if the very act of sharing your story is not a weakness, but the greatest act of power you can ever claim? What if the rough edges of your past are not something to be hidden, but a testament to your incredible resilience?

This book is a revolution in that very idea. It's an invitation to dismantle the walls you've built around your heart, not by force, but with the gentle light of understanding. It's a space where every tear is a prayer and every poem is a testament to survival. Within these pages, you will not find a formula for instant healing or a checklist for "fixing" yourself. Instead, you will find an ally—the author—who has walked a path not unlike your own and has emerged not unscathed, but with a heart full of empathy and a spirit determined to light the way for others. The author has taken the shards of a broken past and shaped the fragments into something unexpectedly whole.

This is a journey of turning pain into purpose, and it is told with a vulnerability that will make you feel as if you are sitting with a trusted friend, sharing a cup of coffee or tea on a white sandy beach, looking at the sunset, somewhere in the Caribbean.

I first met the author twelve years ago, at a time when she was in a different part of her journey.

There was a raw energy about her, a quiet strength that spoke volumes even before she shared her story. She had a way of seeing the world in metaphors and emotions, of translating the invisible architecture of trauma into something tangible and beautiful. Through her poetry, I saw not just a person who had suffered, but a soul who had learned to breathe new life into the very air around her. I saw the power of faith not as an abstract concept, but as a lifeline, a steady hand to pull her from the depths. And I saw resilience not as a grand, dramatic comeback, but as the quiet, daily act of choosing to walk with God and show up for herself, and others, over and over again. This book, born from years of quiet reflection and courageous expression, is the culmination of that journey. It is a testament to the fact that healing does not follow a stopwatch. It's an unfolding, slow and deliberate process of self-discovery and forgiveness.

The author masterfully uses poetry as a tool for this unfolding. Each stanza is a key, unlocking a door you may have thought was sealed shut. They give names to the nameless pains and colors to the colorless voids. They show you how to find the sacred in the mundane, how to see the divine in your own reflection, and how to use your voice—perhaps for the first time—to articulate your own truth.

The journey you are about to embark on within these pages will meet you exactly where you are.

Whether you are a young adult just beginning to process your past, a middle-aged survivor who thought it was too late to heal, or an elder who has carried a lifetime of unspoken burdens, this book is for you. The author's message is a timeless one: that self-love is not a luxury, but a birthright. That your journey is art in progress. The book reminds you that your identity is greater than your past experiences, but the brilliant, multifaceted being you were always meant to be.

The personal stories and lessons woven throughout this book are not just anecdotes; they are lifelines. They are proof that the principles of faith and resilience, when applied with an open heart, can transform the most desolate landscapes of the soul. The author shares their own struggles with finding their voice, their own moments of doubt and despair, and their victories, both big and small. These shared experiences create a safe harbor for your own reflection. As you read, you might find yourself nodding in recognition, a powerful and validating feeling. You might find a single line of poetry that resonates so deeply it feels like a revelation. This is where the magic happens—where the author's story becomes a part of your own healing narrative.

This is a book about the boldness to imagine tomorrow differently. It's a reminder that your truth is not something to be silenced or hidden, but a source of power to be wielded for the greater good. The author has done the courageous work of turning inward, of confronting their own shadows, and they have emerged with a profound understanding of what it means to be whole. Now, they are extending a hand, inviting you to do the same.

The beauty of this book is in its compassionate realism. It doesn't promise a perfect, pain-free life. It acknowledges that the journey of healing is full of stumbles and setbacks. But it holds your hand through every one of them. It shows you that even in the darkest moments, there is a flicker of light—a word, a feeling, a memory—that can be fanned into a flame. It teaches you that your tears are not weakness, but a cleansing release washing away the old so that the new can emerge.

For those who have felt voiceless, this book is a megaphone. For those who have lost hope, it is a beacon. For those who have forgotten their worth, it is a compass. The author has created something truly special, a sanctuary in written form where you can lay down your burdens and pick up the tools you need to build a life of purpose, joy, and profound self-love. I am honored to stand beside this work and to be among the first to welcome you into its embrace. It is my deepest hope that as you turn these pages, you will not only find the words that you needed to hear, but you will also rediscover the strength of your own voice, waiting patiently to be set free.

With all the love in the world,
Neriah LeBlanc

INTRODUCTION

Growing up, a song became my anchor in a silent storm of loneliness: "I'm Nobody's Child," released in 1969 by Karen Young. This song is the inspiration for the title of this book. It was more than music; it was a mirror to my own heart, giving voice to the pain of feeling motherless, fatherless, and voiceless. It was my escape, a deeply personal anthem that gave me a place of belonging when I felt I had none.

I wrote this book in hopes of helping others who have felt this way. I always listened to that song, feeling as if Karen

Young knew me and was singing about my hurt and pain. For once, I didn't feel invisible. She was truly an angel in disguise. God used her and her gift to minister to me through her song. My favorite part was the line, "Just like a flower, I'm growing wild. Nobody loves me, I'm nobody's child." She took the words right out of my mouth because I felt like I was nobody's child. Have you ever felt abandoned like you were nobody's child?

I chose my title, "Nobody's Child," because of that song's profound impact on me. I have never heard any other song that would stop me in my tracks and compel me to stand still and listen to every word. That's what it did to me. I felt like she was singing about me. Every word sung described everything that I was going through and how I felt growing up. I felt invisible and faced so much hatred from the woman who brought me into this world. There's a special bond that a mother and her child have that I didn't have with my mom. The way she looked at me, spoke to me, and treated me was far beyond hate. It was just so evil. Nothing I did was ever good enough for her. Everything I did was always criticized and ridiculed. It was as if she wanted to find a way to beat me or to justify her abuse towards me. I felt unwanted, unloved, and voiceless.

All my life I longed for that special hug and touch from my mom, which I never got. Even when she got sick and had a stroke, I was responsible for all of her financial obligations to pay for her caretakers and the nursing home. I had to swallow my pride and show her love despite her lack of love and respect for me. I had to bite my tongue and swallow my pride for 24 years until she passed away in August 2023.

I remember back in 2003 when I took her from Jamaica and had her come to the Grand Cayman Island to spend some time with me and my family. As I was bathing her after she peed on herself, I couldn't fight back the tears and the emotions. I finally had the courage to ask her why she treated me the way she did, and that was the first and last time she gave me an apology. She stated, "she doesn't know why she did what she did to me and that she's truly sorry." That was the only time she apologized. Since that day, while living with me, she refused to look me in my eyes. She tried to avoid me as much as she was able to.

In my journey of healing and discovering my identity, I learned that my mother probably felt like she, too, was nobody's child. She only operated how she knew how, based on her experience and outlook on life. I am a strong believer that when you know better, you do better. My mom didn't know better. At least that's what I had to tell myself to justify my understanding and try to make sense of why she treated me the way she did.

My intention in writing this book was to share a collection of my poems that are near and dear to my heart, my story as a testimony, and lessons to inspire healing and purpose. You can rise from being and feeling like "Nobody's Child" to a queen. God gave me beauty for my ashes. I began to love myself and have peace that I am God's Child. I am chosen. I am worthy. I am beautiful. I am enough. I am somebody's child.

SECTION 1

CHILDHOOD PAIN
AND ABANDONMENT

Abandon But Never Alone
Sharon Spencer

ﷺ

My nappy not changed, body with mange.
A child without a name, Mama your maim.
We never connect, due to the neglect.
My tears passed you by, unseen, unheard.
Was my pain so well disguised?
Did the blood not stain your sight?
You bruised my fingers, my toes, my back.
Each cut a question left unanswered.
Am I... the peel you tossed aside?
The part of the fruit you never tasted?
Abandoned and alone.
Bare feet, tattered clothes, hair undone.
Yet you rush past like a cheetah breezing by a billboard.
But the Good Samaritan stopped—gosh,
A great big heart with a "what would Jesus do."

No charge, no debt, no shame to me.
He whispers, "My child, have no fear, I do care."
Hallelujah! I now have a brother, a father, a friend.
Arms that hug and hold with eyes that see.
I am somebody's child, big, bold, and bright.
Grace and mercy found me on the side of the road.
Abandoned, yes... but never alone.

Orphan by Cruel Design
Sharon Spencer

Granny loved in a language I do understand.
All day long, comforting and singing her sweet song,
"Jesus loves the little children..."
I felt cared for and loved; now she is gone.
Mama loved in a language like bitter gall.
All day long, yelling and cussing with her big mouth.
I am not cared for; she hates what she bought.
In her disdain, I am caught.
Nine-month package, labeled, "keep and care for life, do not return to sender."
A child is not a cat or a dog, Mama, please, do remember,
a bond for life, no chance to dismember.
Mama speaks recklessly, spreading lies, to look good in her peers' eyes.
Your touch, your words, a child will always remember.
Hog plums my next of kin, green, ripe, or rotting.
Nobody cares to touch, eat, or store.
In life's cruel game, we are left wanting something more.
Life sometimes can be an angry waltz; we're often forgotten.
I am embarrassed and belittled, ugly and blind, nobody's child.
God help me not to become Mama in word, thought, or deed; please keep it on
file.

Ugly Words
Sharon Spencer

You claimed I am not your child.
This was truly astonishing; it blew my mind.
Could there be an underlying reason for this animosity?
Why do you feel this way about me? I am in your shadow,
lost and longing to be free.
I am seeking my mother's attention, not her harsh words or lack of maternal
attention.
The bond is broken, the emotion displaced.
Your mission accomplished, I feel confused and betrayed.
Hurt and angry, do you feel me?
You are amused by my abuse.
The scars unseen, the pain let loose.
I cloaked my pain behind my veil.
Your bitter words will forever alter my life course.
What have I done? What are your desired outcomes?
Seeking freedom, longing for calm.
Do you understand my fear and anxiety?
Sadness and depression,
Your mission accomplished, I feel lonely and weary, guilty and ashamed.
Do you understand my pain?
Mother is a painful word for me.
Father may have hurt you, but why do I have to bear the brunt?
Please, Mom, draft me the wind for my wings so I can soar as an eagle,
unbroken and unbound.
I am a stranger in your eyes, forever unseen,
never the child I have always been.
This is not how a mother should treat her child.
Your mission accomplished, leaving me confused and betrayed.

Mom, do you see me? Can you hear my plea?

In a district called Rose Hill in Summerfield

It was October 1962 in Summerfield, Chapelton, Clarendon, Jamaica, when I entered this world, born to a mother just seventeen.

I often imagine the whirlwind of emotions she must have felt. A young girl cradling a life she hadn't yet learned to guide.

My father, I would later discover, had gone to live in the UK before I drew my first breath, and it wasn't until I turned twenty-nine that I saw him for the first time.

By then, I had grown into years he had missed.

It was my mother's grandmother, my great-grandmother, whom I lovingly called Granny P. A woman rooted in pride and principle, she claimed my supposed father had once worked for her and was, in her eyes, too poor.

"No poor man can own a child under my roof," she declared.

So she gave me her surname, not as a rejection, but perhaps as protection, her own way of claiming me, of anchoring me to something steadfast.

My mother had a quiet friendship with an Asian man who owned the shop in the square. A man with thoughtful eyes and hands that always seemed to offer more than he took. Granny, perhaps out of hope or pride, clung to the belief that I was his.

She longed for a story with edges, one where my roots would bloom from a man who wasn't poor. A man with the presence, stability, and a storefront to his name. He lingered in the shadows for a period of my early childhood, passing by on a gentle Sunday stroll. His smile was carved with a kindness I didn't yet know how to name.

Each week I walked to his shop, and without words, he filled my bag with groceries.

Rice, flour, maybe a sweet tucked in the corner. It wasn't grand, but it was his way of showing. Not as a father, not fully claimed. But as something more than a stranger.

He fell ill and moved away. I cannot forget him, for I carry his name like a shadow stitched into me.

My Mother's Pregnancy at 17

At seventeen, my mother found herself in a situation she never imagined.

Pregnant by a thirty-one-year-old married man, her world was turned upside down. In the small community of Rose Hill in Chapelton, news of her pregnancy spread like wildfire, and it did not take long for the whispers and judgment to follow.

Her father and grandmother were devastated. The disappointment and anger were too much for her to bear.

Her father visited infrequently, sometimes only once a year, her mom a ghost that left a void in her life. My mother lived with her paternal grandmother from a baby, never having met her own mother.

Her paternal grandmother treated her without love; there was no warmth and love in her house.

Her grandmother only saw my mother's mistakes and didn't care about her feelings.

My mother spent her days carrying sugar cane, cocoa, and other produce from the farm to the house for the market, working from dusk till dawn with little or no break and often without a proper meal. Her grandmother was abusive, punishing her harshly for small offenses.

My mother would spend long nights standing in a corner, holding her right ear with her left hand and her right foot with her right hand, unable to sleep. She feared her grandmother, as she would check through the night to see if my mother was complying with her punishment.

Sometimes her grandmother's friend interfered, telling her grandmother to beat my mother first, and then they would tell her the offense. Her grandmother, following their advice, would carry out the punishment before even knowing what my mother had supposedly done wrong.

Despite the harsh home conditions, my mother held on to a dream to become a nurse. But with a baby on the way and unable to attend school, this dream seemed far out of reach.

She was not looking forward to having this baby, as it seems that since the pregnancy, her life had become more unbearable with her grandmother's cruel words and bad behavior towards her.

Nine months later, I was born. She felt so much resentment towards me. The sight of me reminded her of her mistakes and all the pain she had endured. She found it hard to bond with me. She neglected to feed and change me, which caused her grandmother to ask her to leave the house. My mother was happy to leave me in her grandmother's care.

She wanted a better life without all the beating and belittling by her grandmother.

Although I was told that my Granny P had been cruel and unkind to my mother, the woman I knew growing up was nothing like that. Until I was twelve, she treated me like a princess, gentle, loving, and attentive. Her warmth toward me stood in stark contrast to the stories I'd heard about how she treated my mother. It's a complex truth I've carried, trying to reconcile the two very different versions of the same person.

As my mother left home and began building her life, she realized a shocking truth: her birth was never registered, and the name she had been using wasn't a government-registered name. This revelation made her feel even more unloved and neglected, as if her parents and grandmother didn't care enough about her to take the steps to register her birth.

Over the next ten years, my mother worked hard washing people's clothes until she got a job as a cook at a restaurant and later as a worker at a chicken farm located in St. Catherine, Jamaica.

Spending the first twelve years with my great-grandmother, who I affectionately called Granny P, made my mother a stranger to me. My thoughts drifted off to the happier days that were filled with laughter. My Granny P was overprotective and would call my name constantly to check on my whereabouts to make sure I was close by. I used to run around the yard playing or just talking with friends. Granny P's house was by the river where we washed dishes, pots, our clothes, bathed, and fetched water for drinking. We had no refrigerator, no electricity, television, or radio. At night, Granny P would tell interesting stories about her travels. She taught me to say the Lord's Prayer. There was no hostility, just me and Granny loving each other.

We did not have much, but we were happy. She was gentle and loving in her ways towards me. My Granny P never beat me or even yelled at me. She was the true definition of gentleness. To this day, I can tell where I got my gentle demeanor from her. She treated me like I was her world and a princess. She used to always read me a Bible story before going to bed.

She would tell me stories of her trips to different districts to buy coconuts. She used to have a business creating coconut oil, a farm with lots of fruit trees, and a boiling house that makes sugar from sugar cane.

She owned the farm with her husband, Jeremiah Ricketts, who died in the late '40s. She carried on the farm until the 1960s when her health was failing, mainly her eyesight, and it was very difficult for her to manage this farm on her own. She planned to lease it to a well-known butcher who lived in the community.

What my granny didn't know was that this butcher was a dishonest man who wanted to scavenge the lumber from her plantation to sell and had no plan to pay her any money for the lease. Our standard of living began to become unbearable as there was no money for food or medicine.

She would send me at the end of each month to see this butcher for the lease money, and each time he would send me home with a message to tell Granny P that he would pay her next week. However, when next week came, he would say the same thing. After a while, Granny did not send me back to his house; she told me not to worry, that God would provide.

The neighbors would give us food, or sometimes I would go to the farm and cut bananas and take them back home to try and prepare a meal for us to eat.

The bad news was sent by telegram to my grandfather, who lived miles away, that we needed help. I heard my mother lived in May Pen, a town close by.

I got the opportunity to be taken by my Godmother, who was our neighbor, to see my mom for two Christmases. She worked at a Chinese restaurant as a cook. I was about 8 or 9 years old at this time. She looked at me but never hugged, smiled, or said anything to me. I thought to myself, "If I had just met my daughter for the first time, I would be so happy to see her," but it seems my mama was not even happy to see me.

After these two visits with her, she started coming to Rose Hill to see my granny and me and planned for my godmother to start cooking for us and to take care of our clothes washing. Every time my mama visited, I would get a beating for every news someone gave her about my noncompliance with house duties, etc. Growing up, I hated her and her visits, as I became fearful and anxious whenever I got wind of her upcoming visit.

When my identity was revealed:

My great-grandmother was overprotective and so afraid for me to attend school because she was afraid I would hurt myself or someone would hurt me. She had no form of transportation to take me to school, so she would rather keep me home. She would homeschool me until the age of seven. After the neighbors begged and pleaded with her, she finally gave in and allowed me to go to school with the other kids in my community.

I went to school at six years old in 1968. Even that morning, Granny P was still not sure, but I was so excited that when the neighbor and her daughter were ready to go, she simply could not keep me home. I had no birth certificate, so no one was sure about my age or my identity. One neighbor said I was born in 1961, as far as she can remember, because her son was a baby at the time of my birth and he was born in 1960. It was pure speculation. My granny called me Mary, and my supposed father's last name was Hutchinson. So there my name was Mary Hutchinson. I was accepted without my birth paper after my situation was explained to the head teacher.

School was a joyful time, filled with excitement and encouragement from everyone around me. I picked things up quickly and soon became known as a gifted reader and speller. The older folks were always eager to see what I could do—they handed me books, letters from their loved ones abroad, or words just to watch me read or spell them aloud with ease. It felt like I was their performer, and I loved every moment of it.

When I graduated from infant school, it was time to go to all-age school, which was much further from where I live. It was the same procedure in which I was accepted into the school without a birth certificate. Everything seemed to be moving smoothly. It was announced that students in my class were required to bring their birth certificates to school in order to register for the Common

Entrance Exam. Students who passed this exam would be eligible for placement in a high school. Any student who failed to submit their birth certificate by the deadline would lose the opportunity to take the exam.

That afternoon I went home excited. Getting to sit and take this prestigious exam was a dream come true. I ran the last few yards to my home, out of breath, telling my grandma what the teacher said about me taking my birth certificate to school. In a split moment, I came back to earth. "I don't know where your birth certificate is, child," my grandma said. Excitement turned to panic. I looked at my granny several times with disbelief. I had to concentrate and help granny drag her memory to the location of my birth paper. Did my mother take it? Did granny place it in her trunk of papers and don't remember? I need help fast; maybe the neighbors could help. My home was only a couple of yards to the nearest neighbor. "Granny, can I go ask my godmother?"

"No," my granny said with a firm face.

Morning came soon enough, and I realized that Granny was hiding something or was afraid of something. I allowed only one thought: finding my birth paper at all costs. I started asking questions to the neighbors. One neighbor decided to send and ask my grandfather's wife, who lived miles away. An answer had to come soon. I kept thinking, "The deadline is approaching fast for the submission of my birth paper." School was not the same; I was so preoccupied all the time with this issue at hand.

It did come, days after the deadline, from my grandfather's wife who had the birth certificate all along. I was in shock. Who is Sharon Yee Ricketts?

All my eleven years I was Mary Hutchinson. This is a terrible mistake, and I have to be dreaming. But my mother's name is on the birth certificate. Did she have another child, and this is that child's name?

My granny broke the silence. "That is your name, child. I gave that name to you myself."

"A Cemetery Walk": A Reflection on Childhood Fear and Danger

It was about 11 o'clock at night, and I was traveling from my cousin's grocery shop. I had to walk from the grocery shop through another family member's property, which had a cemetery where a few of their family members were buried. My great-grandmother, who was blind, was home alone.

I walked through the pitch-dark night; the darkness felt like a suffocating blanket, pressing down on me. Finally, I reached home. As I started climbing the steps to our house, I opened the door to the room that Granny P and I shared, though we slept in separate beds. We did not have electricity, so there was no light to switch on. The only light in the room was a kerosene oil lamp that rested on a table.

I was shocked to see a young man in my small bed, made from a clothes trunk, a board, and a few blankets. I screamed and shouted to my great-grandmother that there was a man in the room and he was lying in my bed.

My heart raced and my hands trembled as I backed away from the bed. "Get my machete!" my grandma shouted, her voice trembling with fear. I could hear the desperation in her voice, even though she couldn't see the terror in my eyes.

The man's scent lingered in the room, familiar yet out of place. He grabbed at my dress, and I moved away quickly, my mind racing. I shouted for the neighbors, my voice breaking with panic. The person on my bed was a young man whom I now recognized. He was the same one who often played dominoes and board games next door. The sight of him in my bed made my heart stop. He told us to stop shouting and demanded that I lie down in the bed and perform sexual acts on him, promising to reward me with twenty-five cents. His voice was eerily calm, a stark contrast to the panic rising within me.

I made no move towards him. He got up and tried to grab at me, but I was able to move away from him quickly. My heart raced and my hands trembled as I backed away.

I started stepping backwards, shouting for the neighbors. I fled so quickly that I fell down the stairs. The fall left me bruised and aching, but the pain was nothing compared to the fear that gripped me.

I picked myself up, my body aching from the fall, and ran like a cheetah fleeing from a lion. The darkness draped me, but I did not care. I could feel the adrenaline pumping through my veins, propelling me forward as I sprinted towards the neighbor's house, my heart pounding with desperation.

My shouting woke the neighbors, and they came running like the wind from a hurricane. My voice trembled as I explained what had happened, the words barely escaping my lips between sobs.

The neighbors stormed towards my house like a pack of determined bounty hunters, but the young man had vanished, disappearing into the night like a ghost in the wind. The next day, we learned that the young man had left for the city, escaping on a market truck bound for Kingston. The weight of the previous night's terror still clung to me, but the incident was never reported to the police. The silence felt suffocating, as if the unspoken words and unreported crime were a heavy burden we all carried. The injustice of it all lingered, a constant reminder of the fear and danger that had invaded our home.

SECTION 2

MOTHERHOOD AND DISCONNECTION

No Connection
Sharon Spencer

کچھ

I carried my wounds like a whisper in the wind.
The sounds of the past I wish not to restore.
The weight of confusion in his eyes
Causes my heart to be heavy with silent cries.
Through nights of remorse and silent anguish,
I fear the vow I cannot keep.
His gaze my eyes cannot meet.
Shattered glass reflected a broken past,
Yet, hope remained steadfast under my mask.
I found strength in murmured prayers.
A promise kept, a vow unbroken.
To love, protect, I will start afresh.
With each lullaby, I will erase the echoes of a past message.
A love, a touch, I will stitch this wound that hurt so much.
Not with perfection, but with God's grace,

A bond tighter than peas in a pod.
Healed mother, unbroken pane.

My Move to Live in May Pen with My Mother

As a child, I was powerless to the emotional and physical abuse of my mother.

Her abuse towards me ignited years of anger and resentment. Granny P used to speak about my mom a lot when we were together. She told me mama didn't care or love me; that's the reason she didn't come to see me. However, she still told me it was important for me to establish a good relationship with my mother, regardless of her bad behavior towards me.

I felt a tap on my shoulder. "Why are you crying?" my aunt asked with concern in her eyes. It was December of 1974, at the age of twelve (12), when my biological mother came to take Granny to my grandfather's house and for me to live with her. My grandfather insisted that my mother take me to live with her, as he was worried about my safety. I was left with Granny from a baby and only remember seeing my mom about five times. All visits were unpleasant; she hit and cursed at me. I had grown to love Granny; she was all I had for eleven years of my life. She loved and spoke to me softly and with respect. I had a gut feeling that things would not be a bed of roses with my mother, as she swore and cursed at Granny a lot. She had clearly demonstrated that she had no place or fondness for caring for a daughter she abandoned years ago. My grandfather insisted that she take me, as Granny's health was failing and because of the incident that had happened a few months earlier when a known man tried to rape me.

"Sit properly, girl. Your father is in England and doesn't care about you. If you give me any problems, I will break your neck." Coming from a mother who barely knew me, this was frightening. She seemed so angry with everyone. My first eleven years in a different environment had not prepared me to cope, understand, or respond to the new treatment that I encountered. For years, I was shy, nervous, and depressed, facing a new school and new people. I was born with squint eyes (cross-eyes), and the kids at school jeered at me constantly. My mom used it whenever she cursed and beat me.

So, I tried my best to be obedient and follow all her rules. I did well in school, did house chores, and spoke when spoken to and not before. The more I tried, the more she resented me. Whenever I did the laundry, she always found a fault—that the clothes didn't look or smell clean—and would rub them in the dirt and demand that I wash them again. She did the same with the dishes, throwing everything from the dish drainer—pots, plates, and spoons—outside in the dirt. I even remember her beating me in my sleep if she thought I didn't clean them well enough.

Granny P and my grandfather were living over twenty miles away, and we were now living apart for two years. She taught me to read the Bible and would tell me Bible stories prior to bedtime. Boy, how I enjoyed her bedtime stories. I missed her daily; I wished that things could go back to the way they were.

In December 1976, my world shattered. I received the worst news of my life: My beloved Granny P had passed away, and I was devastated. Ever since she had moved in with my grandfather, I had not been able to visit her as often as I wanted. But I held onto a dream that, once I turned 18 and started working, I'd get my own apartment and bring Granny P to live with me. That dream died with her.

Sleep became impossible after the news; the grief was relentless.

At her funeral in January of 1977, I was a wreck. I couldn't hold back the tears. I kept asking, "Why? Why did God take her from me?" She was my everything. The one person who made me feel safe, loved, and understood was now gone.

My school was about nine miles away from home. The school did not have a bus, so most students traveled from a distance and took public transportation, which at times could be unreliable. If I got home an hour or an hour and a half late from the school closing time, my mama would curse and beat me without mercy.

I remember my mother once mentioning that she noticed I came home early from school when I was menstruating and stayed out later when I wasn't. In her tone, I sensed more than just observation; I felt the sting of judgment. To me, it implied something deeper, something hurtful. That remark, along with others just as subtle, carried a heaviness that lingered. It's hard to understand why someone meant to protect your heart would be the one to bruise it.

I began to feel that if I died by hurting myself, it would be better than continuing to live in this misery. I thought about it but did not have the courage to harm myself. If I didn't jump to my mama's every beat, she would curse at me, telling me with the most expletive curse words that I was a "stupid cross-eyed girl" and my "lip hangs down like a jackass under a cool shade." She would constantly rant about how much she hated me and how ugly I was.

I reached a point where I started believing at times these things she was saying about me must be true. However, I took up the habit of reading any material I could find, and I also joined the library. With reading, I could escape and ride along with the characters in my book. Sometimes I imagined that I was Cinderella and that, like her, my situation would change for the better. I pretended to be a twin and would talk to myself as she and I would, happy with my daydreaming of a better life. I would never speak to anyone about my home situation. Instead, I pretended or lied that my mother had died.

From the moment I moved in with my mother, our neighbor welcomed me with kindness. Her warmth felt like sunshine in a shadowed place. She often told me how beautiful I was, words that made me feel like I mattered, like a princess in a story I'd almost forgotten. She gently encouraged me to hold my head high and not absorb the harshness of my mother's words. I found comfort in her presence. In many ways, she became a quiet friend, someone who saw the good in me when I struggled to see it myself.

One afternoon, I stopped by her home, unaware that my mother had returned. Her anger arrived like a storm. She lashed out, demanding to know what I'd said about her. The slap she gave me left me with more than just physical pain; it left silence in its wake. For days I carried the pain without complaint, even as she withdrew from me, refusing to answer when I tried to speak to her with love. When I went back to school, I couldn't concentrate on anything. I thought about the fear of going home in the evening. I hated evenings because I feared going home.

Things would be peaceful for one minute and then, without a signal, it could change. Something as small as a shoelace not tied properly could trigger my mother into a rage of curse words and verbal and physical abuse. Everything, according to her, was my fault. For example, if she lost a pin, she would turn the house upside down, cursing and accusing me of moving her pin. Most of the time, the pin was sitting right on her dress. Not even an apology would be given. This type of behavior continued over the years of living with her.

I though mothers were supposed to be a good and kind influence on their children. I believe there was supposed to be a bond that binds a mother and child together.

I cried often; I was very disappointed with my mother's treatment towards me. This life with her was a nightmare that I desperately wanted to wake up from. I realized when it started but was not certain when or how it would end.

I recalled saying "Mama," this was a new word for me, and she told me in a hostile tone, "I never want to hear you call me mama. For you, my name is Dawta." She refused to let many people know she had a daughter.

I believed something was terribly wrong with my mom. Her behavior was that of a person with multiple personalities. She needed to be in control; every privilege I was supposed to have as a child, she took away. She was so starved for control she kept me away from anyone she thought cared about me. I wasn't allowed to talk to my classmates outside of school. If I happened to see someone I knew while walking down the street and my mother was with me, I had to act like I didn't recognize them. She often accused me of sharing details about our home with outsiders, even when I hadn't. It was one of the ways she kept me isolated, cut off from friendships and connection.

I could not embrace life with laughter and joy like the other kids. I felt like I was in a net and there was no way out. Is this the way a child is supposed to feel—aged, tired, and neglected by the one who gave them life? Nobody's Child.

My Surrogate Family

One day my mother took me to visit one of her closest friends. Her friend had children, and as fate would have it, one of them attended the same school as I did, and we eventually became friends.

That visit marked the beginning of something special. I began going to their home regularly, usually to deliver money from my mother for "pardner savings," which is a traditional, informal community-based savings practice often found in the Caribbean. Over time, I was welcomed with warmth, kindness, and generous hospitality—beautiful words, delicious meals, and a sense of belonging that caught me off guard.

I could not help but feel confused. Why was this family of strangers showing me such love and care when my own mother often treated me with cruelty and indifference?

As the years passed, they naturally became my surrogate family. I visited frequently, spent nights there, and at one point, even lived with them. Outside the bond I shared with Granny P, this family became my haven. They were my safe space, my emotional anchor, and my consistent source of support. Through my early teens and even into adulthood, they've always treated me like one of them.

Runaway from Home

The moment that everything changed for me felt like a light bulb flickering on: sudden, sharp, and undeniable.

My mother had applied to renew her passport using our old address; we had moved from this address a week later. When the passport didn't arrive on time, she exploded. She blamed me for the delay, accusing me of not putting the proper address on the return mail. Her anger turned physical; she cursed at me and beat me as if I were the reason for her frustration.

The very next day, she came to my school and humiliated me in front of everyone. She tried to take off the new shoes she had bought for me, right there in public, just to make a point.

That was the final straw.

Later, she checked with the main post office and found out what had really happened: the postman had delivered the passport to the old address, where it went unclaimed. He then returned it to the post office as undelivered mail. It had nothing to do with me.

That night, after everything that had happened, my mother threw me out of the house.

It was raining hard. I found some cardboard, laid it down on the front porch, and curled up to sleep. The cold soaked through me, but I had nowhere else to go.

In the middle of the night, I was jolted awake by my brother's voice, shouting at me to get off the porch. I didn't move as I was exhausted, soaked, and defeated. Moments later, he called our mother. She stormed out and pushed me off the porch into the pouring rain, telling me I had no right to sleep there because I wasn't the one paying the rent.

I stood there shivering in the dark, soaked to the bone, not just by rain but by the weight of being unwanted.

My mother has always favored my brother, and he knows it. He uses that power to stir trouble for me, knowing she'll take his side every time.

But even after the truth came out, no apology was given to me. Not for the beating, not for the public humiliation, not for the false blame.

I realized I couldn't keep living like this.

So I packed a few clothes and made the decision to run away. I needed to reclaim my peace, my dignity, and my sense of self. The thought of escaping my home, a place that felt like torment, brought a strange sense of peace to my mind. My maternal grandfather and his wife loved me. They didn't have much, but they offered warmth, kindness, and a safe place to be.

I waited patiently for the moment. When my mother left for the market and my brother headed off to school, I quietly packed a few pieces of clothing and took my lunch money. My destination was my maternal grandparents' house.

As I left, I felt a flicker of satisfaction, but my heart was heavy. Fear crept in. What would happen when my mother discovered I was gone? Thoughts of her anger and punishment swirled around my head, bringing tears to my eyes. But I reminded myself, I had to be strong.

I discovered something strange after crying; I felt strength rising in me, a kind of resolve I hadn't known before. At just fourteen (14) years old, I understood that if my life was going to change, it was up to me.

During the bus ride to my grandparents' house, my mind was in turmoil. Sadness and confusion battled within me. I kept asking myself: why should a daughter have to run away from her own mother? I was so lost in thought that I did not even notice the tears running down my face, until a few passengers looked over and gently asked, "Why are you crying?"

Compared to the hustle and bustle of May Pen, Vere felt like a calm retreat. Life there was quieter, and the people were noticeably more kind and welcoming. My grandparents embraced me without hesitation, offering love, acceptance, and zero judgment. They were aware of how my mother treated me and had tried to confront her about it before, but she always deflected responsibility, placing the blame squarely on me.

Only a few hours after I arrived at my grandparents' home, a relative shouted that my mother was at the gate. Panic surged through me, and I quickly ran to hide in a nearby tree so she wouldn't realize I was there.

She launched into a dramatic tale, claiming someone had seen me in Mandeville with a young baby, leaning against a taxi. My grandparents listened patiently, but they didn't believe a word of it. They refused to tell her that I was there, choosing instead to shield me with their quiet protection.

Her frustration turned bitter. Upset that they didn't support her accusations, she stormed off, leaving behind a chilling promise to harm me if she ever found me.

I struggled to respond to the love my relatives offered. My mother had shattered my trust in people, and at times, I felt so unbearably empty it seemed impossible to shake. Reading became my escape; books were the only place I could disappear from reality. But even they couldn't silence the voice of low self-esteem that kept me isolated, always a loner.

I've been thinking about sharing how I feel with my grandmother. She is one of the few who might truly understand.

My maternal grandparents faced financial hardship, and when I moved in with them, I feared I was just another mouth to feed. They never complained, but my young mind internalized every act of kindness and generosity, often feeling undeserving of it. I wore hopelessness like a permanent frown.

One evening, my grandparents sat me down. They encouraged me to give my mother another chance and return to live with her. My mother promised to treat me better this time, and my aunt agreed to rotate holiday stays with her to support me. During those times, I'd continue spending time with my grandparents, my quiet anchors.

"I desperately wanted to die. I'm nobody's child. Just like the flowers, I'm growing wild," I recalled from the song. The songwriter must have known about me.

RETURNING HOME AFTER RUNNING

I used to run away from my mama's house quite often. This time, I remember heading home and being escorted by my aunt to my mama's home. The closer I got to my mother's house, the more nervous I became. This was my worst nightmare come true. Just a few more minutes and we would reach my mother's house.

My grandparents thought it would be best to give my abusive mother another chance to be a better mother to me. As my aunt and I reached my mother's house, I built up courage and stepped inside.

"Hello, Mama," I said. She responded with a cold stare and a curt, "hello."

I hurried towards the room my brother and I had shared before I ran away from home. My younger brother, Mark, was there, and from his cold stare, I realized he wasn't happy about my return.

Feeling so uncomfortable, I decided not to unpack my bag.

The next day I found myself home alone as my mother and brother left without telling me. I enjoyed the solitude; I love reading and talking to myself. I was able to clean and cook dinner before they got home.

Just the sound of her voice reinforced my fear of being back in the house; she could still hurt me. Her cold stare terrified me.

I recalled a few weeks after my return home, my brother Mark stole some money that someone had given my mother to purchase something in Kingston.

I had no idea he had stolen this money until later. My mother came home one evening in a mad rage. I was in the bathroom when I heard her screaming my name and cursing at the same time. I was mortified.

I made a dash from the bathroom, but she caught me by my hair in the passage and started beating me. It hurt so much. I cried and shook uncontrollably. I realized I was bleeding but wasn't sure where.

I weighed about ninety-four pounds, with a lush head of hair and two lanky legs that could barely hold me up, while my mother was about 240 pounds. She was beating me, and I had no idea what offense I had committed. She tore my clothes off, leaving me barely clothed in just my panties with blood running down my face and pooling on the floor.

I thought to myself that if I lay down and stopped breathing, maybe she would think I was dead and stop hitting me.

Through the blood and tears, I heard a familiar voice: "Dawta, stop!" My savior had now arrived; it was my mother's boyfriend.

When my mother saw him, she yelled at him to leave. He pushed past my enraged mother and helped me to my feet, all the while scolding her, "What kind of a mother treats her child like an animal?"

My mother shouted that I had stolen her money. This was the first time I heard what her enraged behavior was about.

I had no idea what money she was talking about, so I sobbed more, as I had not taken any money. My stepfather scolded her for not investigating before beating me so brutally while he got some alcohol and cleaned the cut on my forehead and put a band-aid on it.

Nothing I said could convince her that I had not stolen her money. She told her friends and neighbors that I had stolen her money and that I had learned to steal because I stayed with my grandparents for a few months. I felt ashamed for days, as none of the people she told would even acknowledge me when I greeted them.

A few days after my mother beat me, I discovered the truth about who had taken her money.

While I was outside our home, my brother's friend, who lives next door, called out to me from his yard. He mentioned in our conversation that the ball he was playing with belonged to my brother. He explained that my brother had bought it, and although they played with it together, my brother had asked him to keep it at his house.

That moment, something clicked in my mind. I knew my brother couldn't afford a ball like that. It became clear: he had stolen our mother's money, used it to buy the ball, and let her believe I was the one responsible.

I told my mother what I'd learned, and when she confronted my brother's friend, he confirmed the story. Despite the truth coming out, she never apologized for wrongly accusing me or for the beating I endured because of it.

SECTION 3

SURVIVAL MECHANISMS

Books Transport Beyond the Pain
Sharon Spencer

Papers bind with hard cardboard and bold letters written in ink.
Under the shadow of the cool mango tree, I read the stories of others, carefree
and as rough as a sea,
Where characters begin to dance and breathe,
Their tales of triumph and pain they weave,
And soon the healing has begun.
Through lands where lions fiercely roar, naughty boys took roosters playfully
from their roost, to a land where Cinderella found her Prince.
In books, I find a safe place beyond my tears and pains,
A cherished space, a solace,
A sanctuary.
Each word a board, each line a pen.
Through deep imagination, I gently draw my thoughts within,
In tales of old and dreams anew.

I find a path that leads me through.
With characters that share my plight,
Their murmured strength, a beacon of light. Through books,
I leave my pain behind, and in their worlds,
my comfort find.

Seeing My Dad in Person for the First Time

When I learned that the man who was my father had returned to Jamaica with his wife to retire after living in the UK since 1962, a relative prompted me to visit their house.

I decided to visit their home, although it was miles away. When I arrived, both he and his wife acknowledged me as his daughter; there was no denying the family resemblance.

Years earlier, when I was born, my stepmother had come to my great-grandmother Granny P's house at my father's request, hoping to have him recognized as my dad. But Granny P refused; she did not want a poor man, as she called him, claiming a child in her home.

I didn't meet my father until I was in my late twenties. Despite the time lost, we built a close, beautiful relationship. He apologized for missing my childhood, but I was not looking for explanations; I was a grown woman finally filling a lifelong void. From that moment on, I became daddy's little girl.

He would cook my favorite meals, and we would sit together in the quiet kitchen, talking late into the night. He shared stories of his life in England and introduced me to extended family by name that I never knew I had. Every visit was met with a warm hug and a wet kiss on the cheek, his way of showing love. I can still feel it.

Although we only had a short few years together before he passed, our bond was deep and undeniable. He was proud of the woman I had become, and he made sure I knew it. His friends would often tell me how much he spoke of me, how highly he thought of me. That meant everything to me. I would visit him and his wife while I was on holiday. My stepmother welcomed me and my family with open arms and genuine affection. Both she and my father embraced me fully without hesitation.

Their time was short. My father passed away within ten years of our reunion, and my stepmother followed a few years later. But in that brief window, I experienced a kind of love and understanding that stood in stark contrast to the abusive relationship I had with my mother; the difference was like night and day. Meeting my father and being accepted by him and my stepmother healed something in me. I got to be his baby girl, and that gift will stay with me forever.

Mooney & Skyey
Sharon Spencer

Laughing loudly with hidden tears
Through cane fields and paths so wide
Mooney, Skyey and I raced breathlessly side by side
Steadfast friends through rain and shine
Undeniable bond, partner in crime
A friendship pure through every storm
Two pigs and a girl are not the norm
Their love was real, their love was rare.
No leash, no fence as they led the way.
We played hide and seek as we may
With every run, with every flight
We soared beyond the edge of night
Fun starts again, tomorrow morning bright

SECTION 4

A JOURNEY THROUGH CHALLENGING TIMES

A Mother's Shadow
Sharon Spencer

عهيمو

Your words, bitter as gall, venomous and cold.
A love that stung, a grip that controlled.
Belittled, neglected, I shrink, I doubt.
Lost in a world of silent shouts.
You taught me obedience and fear so well,
To dance to a bark that I dare not steer.
A love with shackles and cruel terms,
A lesson taught to be submissive.
Your hammer and nail—banner mission.
A quiet hissing, I please with ease.
A Peter Potty syndrome and doormat disease,
Afraid that love would slip away fast.
You spat, "I don't need you," red lips fierce.
And still, I rain kisses on the boogie tempest time and again.
Wounds pierce deep as well,
and bleed like a running stream.

I walked beyond the snake's full shade.

And now I roar like the thunderous scream of a lion—not a mare.

And silent the snake rattling

without care or fear.

And perhaps, at last, I walk within my own silhouette.

No Longer Mute
Sharon Spencer

What a mess I am, so stressed.
How can I speak my truth
Without you being a brute?
What triggers the beating
Since the beginning?
Hitting and shouting.
I am not allowed to hear my own
thoughts or my own voice.
How can I speak my truth?
I fear the reaction to my questions.
What I feel I can't even mention.
Longing for liberty, thirsty for light.
Deep down, the furnace burns bright.
To break these shackles, to end this plight,
With every breath, I will gather the strength.

I'll find my voice, I'll muster the might,
To stand tall, to tread the passage.
Silent no longer, voiceless no more,
I will embrace the power of my rebirth.
For I deserved love, I deserved respect.
In the running stream, at last, I see my worth.
If I may say, my fear and pain cease today.

Silent Prayers
Sharon Spencer

In midnight's silence, the shadows creep.
A soul weighs down, too lost to weep,
Calling on Him in desperate need.
A silent prayer, a murmured hymn.

Psalms 91:15
"He will call upon me and I will answer him."
"I will be with him in trouble, and honour him high."
A promise unwavering, I trust His word.
Unspoken prayers, a trembling heart
Through hurricanes, through floods and the devil's snare.

Romans 10:13
"For whoever will call on the name of the Lord will be saved."
I will follow His light that leads up yonder.

Enough is Enough
Sharon Spencer

Enough is enough—I fight, I stand.
No longer bound by prickle hands.
The noise silent, the scars may stay,
But I refuse to live this way.
I gather the strength from broken nights,
From silent echoes, from stolen rights.
No longer weak; I fight with might.
Enough is enough—freedom is mine.
To walk without shackles, free from pain.
The past may whisper, my aim to heal.
Freedom's water upon my face.
It cleanses my soul from all the waste.
No shackles remain, my strength is real.
Enough is enough—my power I take back.

SECTION 5

REDISCOVERY AND HEALING

Communion Sunday

Some relationships arrive as mirrors, reflecting lessons we never expect about ourselves, our past, our pain, and the patterns we unknowingly carry forward. Recognizing those echoes became a turning point, guiding me toward deeper understanding and healing. That new awareness was still fresh on the first Sunday of April 6, 2014, when I woke up with no plan beyond sipping my ginger tea for the knot of pain in my neck and persuading my two boys to keep the television low so I could reset. Yet before that second blink had fully opened, an unshakable tug in my spirit whispered again: *Go to church!*

That Sunday, I had not planned on attending church service as I was not feeling well. However, when I woke up, I found myself speaking my thoughts out loud. "I am going to church later," I said, then immediately contradicted myself. "I am not going later; I'm going this morning." And that was that.

My sons love to stay up late on Saturday nights playing games and hiding away in their rooms. When I woke them up for church, two protested, insisting they weren't going to church as they wanted to sleep. I made it clear I wasn't asking for their opinion; I simply wanted them in the car by the time I finished dressing. They weren't pleased, but they complied.

Before I turned the car key, I walked into my closet, traced my fingers across the vision board I had created at the top of the year that I had pinned next to my sweaters, and breathed a quick prayer. Everything on that board had been placed with intention. I even cleared a portion of my closet and instructed my friends and family not to park any vehicle in a certain section of the front lawn of my house because that spot was designated for my future spouse. I was making space, both physically and spiritually, for something new as a demonstration of my faith. On my vision board, I wrote that I needed a husband who loves God, with a willingness to serve Him, and who loves and respects me. Vision boards require a certain audacity, and audacity was the only form of courage I could manage in those days.

Seemingly out of nowhere, life began to shift.

By the time we reached the church, my boys climbed out of the car as though every limb contained lead. I rushed them toward the front doors; since an earlier surgery, there's a quiet pull in my neck—a subtle nudge to move with care. As I stepped onto the walkway, a voice, unknown and masculine, called from behind: "Excuse me, could you point me to the restroom?"

It reminded me not to twist too quickly, so I turned just enough. However, I walked him halfway to the restroom, then lifted my arm, gestured with my hand, muttered, "Sir, there's the restroom," and kept walking. I felt him follow at a polite distance. I felt something else, too, though I could not name it then, a beam of attention as gentle as winter sunlight on skin. While in church, when the pastor spoke about Communion, I sensed that anonymous gaze land on me again, warm and unhurried. A question posed from behind. Yet I refused to turn. A lifetime of unwanted attention had trained me to keep my eyes forward, my posture guarded.

After church, as members met and greeted visitors, I found myself facing him. Up close, he looked both familiar and entirely new: skin the color of polished cedar, eyes set with a softness I had forgotten men could carry, chef whites crisp beneath a navy blazer. I handed him my business card and asked him to give me a call. I worked as an insurance sales agent, and I was curious to know if he knew the manager or HR of the hotel and would be willing to give me a referral for an appointment to present some of our health plans.

On Monday, he called, and I was unexpectedly excited to hear his voice.

I was sitting at my desk cross-checking new applications when my work phone rang. The moment I heard his voice, a deep calm that stretched each word like honey over bread, my stomach flipped like a startled fish. He told me, quite directly, that he was single and looking for love. My immediate thought: *"Single my foot."* Men always say they're single to get in with a woman they like.

I confessed I was in a long-distance relationship that left my spirit restless, though I'd been praying for clarity. He listened without interruption or rushing. The next day, he called again, this time with an invitation to dinner. I told him I'd check my schedule and let him know. Truthfully, I already knew my schedule, but I wasn't ready to confirm just yet; I didn't want to seem too eager.

I spoke to my boys about it, and to my surprise, they gave me their blessing to accept the dinner date. After texting him to confirm, my sons immediately wanted details, demanding his phone number, the restaurant name, and what time I planned on getting home. Their enthusiasm felt like a prophecy.

Our first date unfolded like a scene I might once have clipped for another vision board. As the sun set, the restaurant hostess, a stranger to both of us, exclaimed, "What a beautiful couple. Celebrating an anniversary?" We laughed awkwardly—the second time we had met—but part of me inhaled the words like oxygen. After dinner, we checked on my boys to assure them I was okay, and then we proceeded to hang out at Seven Mile Beach. We faced the sea and talked until stars quilted the sky. He asked about my sons, my work, my faith; he listened so attentively, which was rare to me. After dinner, when the bill arrived and I offered to contribute, he looked as though I had suggested he sell a kidney. 'No lady has ever reached for the check with me.' We walked to the car glowing from some inner place I had believed was irreversibly broken.

From that evening on, we saw each other after work every single day. We shared childhood traumas, secret dreams, and quiet prayers. I felt like a schoolgirl discovering her first love—except I was fifty-one, with scars older than some fairy tales.

Within a few weeks, we realized that we truly loved each other and wanted to spend the rest of our lives together. He requested a meeting with my church Minister. He explained to the Minister that he intended to marry me, that he valued counseling and accountability, and that he recognized the sacredness of a marital covenant. We breezed through pre-marital sessions, each revelation pulling us closer: he was born in Cayman but raised in New York, returned on a chef's contract yet instantly knew he wanted to stay; he had told his father years earlier he would never marry, and his father had smiled prophetically—"You'll marry when you meet the right one." Prophecy fulfilled. With the blessing of his older sister, my boys, a few close friends, and our pastor, we set a date. Seven weeks from the Sunday I showed him the restroom, on June 14, 2014, we became husband and wife. I wore white lace, my sons stood proudly beside me, and photographs of that day still reflect a joy that lights my face from within.

Not everyone applauded our velocity. Many questioned my motives: What kind of woman marries without a family present? Is she pregnant? Is she hiding something? Why the rush? Others accused me of secrecy because I chose intimacy over spectacle. I understood. People fear what moves faster than their imagination. But we trusted the One who was writing our story. God, after all, had drafted the blueprint long before we recognized the plot of this beautiful life we've now shared for eleven years. I sent wedding pictures the next morning as an answer to rumors. Truth does not need a microphone; it shines on its own.

To understand why this miracle felt so seismic, you must first know the terrain it disrupted. The story stretches far behind the pews, winding through decades of loneliness that taught me to distrust joy. My mother, God rest her soul, had called me ugly, worthless, and unlovable so often that her voice became the one in my head. I believed her. She left me with my granny in rural Jamaica while I was still clingy-kneed, convinced my presence ruined her life. Granny loved me fiercely, but when blindness stole her sight, I became a caretaker at age ten. Nights in our pitch-black yard left me navigating tombstone-lined paths to borrowed suppers, until that evening I returned to find a half-naked stranger sprawled in my bed. My shriek summoned neighbors; the intruder vanished into the darkness, but the terror stayed lodged beneath my sternum. My grandfather insisted my mother reclaim me, but her house was no haven. She left groceries and disappeared sometimes for days, carrying the keys to tenderness with her. My motivation became simple: prove her wrong.

At nineteen, I birthed my first son, and postpartum reality felt cold. My body rejected breastfeeding; when he cried, my womb flared with knife-sharp aches. I interpreted the pain as punishment—another confirmation of my mother's verdict. Seven years later, my second son arrived, and I loved him fiercely yet feared I was already failing him.

In the early '90s, my sisters-in-law helped me find a job opportunity that led me to the Cayman Islands. It was a difficult decision to leave my boys behind, but I entrusted my two boys with relatives, and we cherished the time we spent together during holidays—either they would come to visit, or I would travel back. Being apart from them was very difficult, and every reunion felt both joyful and bittersweet.

Coming to Cayman brought more than just a new beginning; it brought companionship in a man whose story quietly mirrored my own. We found comfort in each other's presence; it was as if life had gently aligned our paths. Over time, the relationship shifted. For years I stayed for the children, for stability, for the hope that things would change. Eventually, we separated.

The separation was not easy. It drained resources and tested my faith. There were moments when help arrived in ways I couldn't explain—just in time, just enough. These moments reminded me that I am not alone. We found a way to co-parent our boys with grace and understanding. Over time, a friendship blossomed between us. Not everything was lost—perhaps we were always meant to walk side by side as friends, not as life partners. Maybe we entered that chapter without first seeking God's guidance.

After the separation, I underwent something deeper than surgery: a stripping away of everything false. I spent two full years learning to love myself—taking myself to dinner, journaling under a breadfruit tree, singing hymns over laundry, paying off my home a year later than my vision board had predicted but paying it off nonetheless. I was forty-nine when I wrote the sticky note that said, "Husband who loves God." Two years and a morning nudge later, he stood behind me in church asking for directions to the restroom.

Living Again

Eleven years have passed since that Communion Sunday. Being loved well still feels like wearing silk after decades of burlap. My husband prays with me before dawn, brings me tea before bed, sings worship songs while seasoning snapper, and calls my adult sons to let them know stew chicken waits on the stove. When he comes home before me, he starts dinner and texts, *Drive safe, Love.* He once told me he fasted for a year from romantic relationships, asking God to prepare him for the wife he would send. The weekend before we wed, he was baptized, declaring he wanted to know the God I serve for himself. When I look at him, I see every bullet point from my vision board made flesh. I show him that board sometimes, tracing my fingers over each photo while tears gather at the bend of my jaw. Audacity, it seems, pleases God.

Living again is not just the presence of new love; it is the absence of fear. My home exhales peace and serenity. Friends stay the night and tell me the atmosphere feels like a resort. Even the dogs seem to bark softer. The first photograph taken after my baptism sits beside an earlier one; side by side, they tell a resurrection story. In the older picture, my shoulders hunch, my eyes are dimmed, and my face is lined beyond my years. In the newer, I look decades younger, washed and rinsed. As a sister at church says, "Like God put you through a washer, then laid you in the sun to dry."

Healing, I have learned, is not a staircase you climb and conquer; it is a spiral you revisit, each time at a higher vantage point. When my mother passed recently, grief reopened old wounds I thought were scarred over. I had to sit with the child inside me who still ached for her approval. I wrote her name in my journal, poured out both sorrow and gratitude, and handed the pages to the Lord. I will always carry echoes of her voice, but they no longer dictate my worth.

People ask what joy feels like after so much sorrow. It feels like waking up eager to go home rather than afraid. It feels like singing "Great Is Thy Faithfulness" while folding towels, the smell of lavender softener rising like incense. It feels like my husband tapping a rhythm on the countertop while I dance barefoot. Joy is not the absence of memory or sorrow; it is the presence of redemption, the refusal to let sorrow have the final word.

Sometimes I catch myself giggling—a full-throated sound that startles me because it had been years since I last laughed this hard. That laugh is evidence. Evidence that guilt lost its grip. Evidence that being fifty-one does not disqualify you from love. Evidence that healing can leave you better, not bitter. Evidence that God can turn a battered neck into a head held high.

If you are reading this and you feel the weight of years or the sting of your past telling you it is too late, hear me: Age is only how long the earth has been blessed with your presence. That's all. It does not limit God's creativity or heaven's timeline. If anything, it qualifies you for a miracle others will call impossible. Vision boards are not childish—write the dream, clear the closet space, park your car with expectation. Audacity is faith wearing heels.

I write now more than ever—poems, children's stories, letters to the woman I was at twenty. In that letter, I tell her: You are stronger than you can fathom. One day you will look back and marvel at the miles God carried you. Your past does not disqualify your future; it fertilizes it. Soar, girl. Writing is how I bleed out the pain without harming myself, how I turn wounds into wells for others. Some parts still tremble on the page. That is okay. Authentic stories cure silent hearts.

And yes, there are days my body aches when the weather shifts, and flashbacks flicker like old film. But peace now sits deeper than pain. I breathe. I pray. I walk outside and let Cayman's turquoise horizon remind me that every storm eventually clears.

Living again is my daily rebellion against every lie spoken over me—my mother's condemnation, society's ageism, my own fearful narratives. I married at fifty-one; I glow brighter at sixty-two than I did at twenty-five; I speak with a voice that may rasp but never wavers. I am not nobody's child. I am God's daughter—beloved, purposeful, unstoppable.

So if you find me on a Monday morning, you will likely see me in my closet, straightening that old vision board—now a framed relic of a fulfilled prophecy—and pinning a new note beside it. Because living again is not the final chapter; it is an open door to chapters yet unwritten. And I, Sharon Yee Spencer, intend to step through every single one—with heels clicking, laughter rising, grace lighting each footfall, and an empty patch of driveway forever reminding me that faith will always find somewhere to park.

Age is Just a Number
Sharon Spencer

Celebrating Love and Happiness at fifty-one.
A life once marked by scars and tears,
At fifty-one, love appears.
The heart knows not of numbered days,
It leaps, it sings, it softly sways.
With moonlit whispers, love takes flight,
Expanding more with each new night.
Hand in hand through time we glide,
With love and laughter as our guide.
Sunrise shines and voices cheer,
A bow to a love that grows each year.
Like a stream strong and happiness grow,
Ageless love that always glows.

SECTION 6

Testimony and Triumph

Living My Best Years
Sharon Spencer

ﮩﻤﮩ

Through battles past and paths unkind,
Where scars once wept but forgiveness grew,
A hope I found, with warm embrace,
A spirit of resilience, a heart of gratitude.
I rise as fresh as the cool summer breeze.
A rose blooms, each petal rises,
A breath of joy upon the sun.
A promise that life will endure,
Like mountains from long ago.
For every thorn upon the rose,
A bud grows brighter—hope is found.
The thorns prick deep, but here I stand,
Like the cotton tree with steadfast roots.
Each root shaped what I embraced.
None of my past hurt went to waste.

Gratitude, resilience, and spirit renew.
Living my best years, high or low.

Looking back over my journey, one moment stands out—a time when everything seemed uncertain, and I was on the edge of losing hope. It was during a difficult financial crisis when I felt completely alone and unsure of my next step.

I had exhausted every option and prayed countless times, and still, there was no clear answer. Then, in the most unexpected way, God showed up. It was not in a loud, dramatic fashion, but in the quiet, undeniable details that proved His presence.

Just when I had given up, a friend called me at my place of work, offering exactly what I needed. The timing was so perfect, the provision so precise, that I knew it couldn't have been a mere coincidence. That moment reaffirmed my faith. It was a reminder that even when I can't see the way forward, He is already making a way.

How Philippians 4:13 Has Grown in Meaning for Me

At first, Philippians 4:13 felt like a simple encouragement—a reminder that I could overcome obstacles with God's help. I saw it as a motivation to push through challenges, to believe that I could achieve anything if I just had enough faith. But as life unfolded, I realized this verse wasn't just about success or personal victories. It was about endurance, about finding strength in Christ when I felt weak, weary, or uncertain. There were moments when I had nothing left, when circumstances felt impossible, and yet, somehow, I kept going. Not because of my own strength, but because God carried me.

Over time, I've come to see Philippians 4:13 as a promise—not that everything will be easy, but that no matter what I face, I won't face it alone. It's a verse that has met me in my lowest valleys and reminded me that even in my struggles, Christ strengthens me.

Now, when I read these words, I don't just see encouragement; I see proof of God's presence in my life. I see the moments when I thought I couldn't make it, but I did. And I know that whatever comes next, His strength will sustain me.

As you're reading this book, I want you to know that I understand where you are right now in your journey. I know the questions racing through your mind, the uncertainty, the weight of waiting for answers. I was there once, too, wondering if things would ever shift, if I'd ever feel strong enough, or if I'd ever truly see God's hand at work in my life. But let me tell you something: everything you're facing right now is shaping you. Every tear, every doubt, every moment where you feel unseen—God sees it. And He is working, even when you can't see the outcome.

You won't stay in this season forever. One day, looking back, you'll realize this moment was essential to your growth and the person you'll become. You have more strength than you know. Keep moving forward, even on the days when it feels impossible. Let go of the weight you no longer need to carry and trust that God is working out something far more beautiful than you can imagine.

If I could go back and talk to myself 20 years ago, I would tell her to breathe—to stop trying to control every outcome and to trust that even in uncertainty, God never fails. I want to remind and reassure you to hold on. You're not alone. Your story is not over. In fact, the best chapters are still ahead.

There were so many invisible victories that unfolded behind the scenes on my journey that outsiders never saw. The days when fear and doubt crept in, but instead of giving in, I whispered a prayer, held onto a promise, and kept believing even when the outcome was unclear.

My Invisible Victories:

Showing up for myself and for my responsibilities, even when people needed me most.

Learning that setbacks are not failures but stepping stones.

Learning that my rest was not a weakness but a renewal.

Choosing to find the good even when circumstances didn't make it easy.

Practicing gratitude for good and bad days.

Letting go of things that do not serve me, not in one big moment, but daily in small ways.

Letting go of resentment, not because they deserved it, but because I refuse to let it weigh me down.

My prayers in private, even when scriptures weren't clear, but still trusting God's plans.

Replacing self-criticism with affirmations, realizing the negative inner dialogue, and rewriting the narrative.

Learning to step away from the noise or any distractions in order to protect my heart and to create boundaries for my well-being.

Realizing that progress isn't only about big wins but also in the quiet, unseen shifts—the nights I did not spiral, the morning I woke up with more hope, the way I handled situations differently than before. These are also small wins that showed my growth.

My Hidden Scars Becoming a Badge of Honor

For a long time, the wounds left by my childhood trauma were something I carried in silence, buried beneath layers of shame and secrecy. The abuse I endured at the hands of my own mother shaped how I saw myself—fragile, unworthy, broken. I tried to hide the scars, fearing that if people saw them, they would see me as less.

But time, growth, and healing have changed that. Now, I see this scar not as a mark of pain but as proof of my resilience. It tells a story—not of defeat but of survival. I endured something that should have shattered me, yet I am still here. Stronger, wiser, and whole.

This scar is no longer something to conceal—it is my **badge of honor**. A testament to my strength I never knew I had.

While my faith in God was my anchor, my church family, friends, therapist, mentors, my husband, and even strangers played an instrumental role in my healing. The moment I realized I couldn't heal alone was when I had a conversation with someone who truly listened, who did not dismiss my pain but saw me in it. A presence that reminded me that I wasn't alone in carrying the weight of my past. They stood with me when the pain felt unbearable, offering patience when I struggled to trust compassion. When my wounds resurfaced, they offered unwavering support even when I doubted my own strength.

The Biggest Misconception About Myself Before Healing

Before healing, the biggest misconception I had was believing that the abuse defined me. That somehow I was undeserving of love, unworthy of kindness, or irreparably broken. Healing revealed the truth: I was never the problem. I was always worthy of love, safety, and respect.

To guard against slipping back into that lie, I recognize that when old wounds whisper, I must surround myself with people who remind me of my true worth, challenge negative thoughts before they take root, and hold on to evidence of my growth. Healing isn't about pretending the past never happened but about refusing to let it control how I see myself today.

In paying it forward and serving others, I offer my support and wisdom to those facing hardship because of my own journey. I have a deep well of understanding for others navigating trauma and healing. Whether through listening, sharing my experience, or simply being a safe space for someone to lean on, I remind others they are not alone. Being a source of strength for my family and friends. The love and care that my husband, friends, and family once extended to me, I return tenfold. I lift those around me, showing them through my presence and actions that love, trust, and kindness can coexist despite the past scars.

Advocating for healing and resilience, whether directly or indirectly, my story serves as proof that healing is possible. I may not even realize it, but just by owning my scars and seeing them as a badge of honor, I inspire others who are still struggling to find their strength.

What surprises me the most is the way my personal healing has rippled outward. How what once felt like a solitary battle has now become a source of empowerment for others. The way my pain has transformed into purpose is a remarkable thing.

Gratitude for me looks like pausing to savor the first sip of tea. Instead of rushing through the morning, I take a moment to appreciate the warmth, the aroma, and the quiet comfort of this simple ritual. Sending a quick text to someone I appreciate—a short, heartfelt message to a friend, partner, or family member—can be a reminder of the love and connection in my life. Recognizing mundane kindness, whether it's stepping outside and feeling the breeze, having a job to go to, or even the rhythm of daily responsibilities. Gratitude and kindness, whether it's a smile at the barista, patience in traffic, or a genuine thank you to a coworker. My engagement with the world often reflects my gratitude.

A Prayer for My Reader:

God, for the one holding these pages, feeling lost, weary, and uncertain, meet them at this moment. Lift their burdens, quiet their fears. Whisper truth into their heart, remind them that even in the depths of despair, they are not alone.

Amen.

Additional 24 x 7 Help Lines & Services in Grand Cayman (Cayman Islands)

Service	What it helps with	Phone (local)	Toll-free/Alt.	Website/ Email	Notes
Cayman Islands Crisis Centre (CICC)	Domestic & intimate-partner violence, sexual assault, stalking	(943-CICC 943-2422)	1-800-534-2422 (from any FLOW/ LIME land-line)	cicc.ky • info@cicc.ky	24-hr shelter "Estella's Place" + on-call advocates who will meet you at the hospital or police station.
Family Resource Centre (FRC) – Department of Counselling Services	Parenting support, safety-planning, free counselling, court accompaniment	949-0006	N/A	frc.gov.ky	Walk-in weekday "Ask-a-Counsellor" clinic (no appointment).
Mental Health Helpline	Crisis anxiety/depression, suicidal thoughts, substance use	1-800-534-6463 (toll-free)	WhatsApp voice: 547-6463	dcs.gov.ky	9 a.m.–10 p.m. daily. Operated by Government Counselling Services clinical team.

Service	What it helps with	Phone (local)	Toll-free/Alt.	Website/ Email	Notes
TAYA Lounge (Children & Youth)	Teens/young adults (14-29) facing abuse, homelessness, family conflict	322-2292	WhatsApp 922-2292	taya@cicc.ky	Free meals, after-school drop-in centre, emergency placement help.
Royal Cayman Islands Police Service – 911	Immediate danger, reporting a crime	911	From mobile: +1 345 949 4222 (non-emergency desk)	rcips.ky	Officers have a Family Support Unit trained in DV & SA cases.
Cayman Islands Red Cross – Protection & Empowerment	Child protection, sexual violence prevention, community training	949-6785	N/A	redcross.org.ky	Free psycho-social first-aid and referrals.

CONCLUSION

FROM PAIN TO PURPOSE

Journaling for Healing

To create journal entries that move me forward, I asked myself, "If no one ever says sorry, can I still heal?" I forgave myself for needing love in places it was never given.

Writing Rituals—the time of day, setting, prompts, or prayers—help journaling feel safest and most honest.

Nighttime journaling: A sacred space for truth

A quiet space without interruption

My favorite pen and notebook

Allowing my tears to flow freely as they are part of my story

Choose five journal prompts you wish someone had given you at the very start of your healing journey:

What pain am I carrying that I've learned to call normal? Sometimes we don't realize the weight we've gotten used to. Recognizing it is the first exhale.

What parts of me have I silenced to fit in, survive, or be loved? This opens the door to reconnecting with the truest version of myself, the one that did not need to shrink.

Am I ready to stop fighting my past and start understanding it? Not to excuse, but to make space for compassion for others, sure, but mostly for me.

How would I show up for myself if I believed I was worthy of tenderness? Because the healing isn't just in the doing; it's in how you do it and whether love is part of the process.

What would it feel like to trust myself again? The journey home is less about finding new answers and more about remembering the voice that I stopped listening to.

FAITH AND AFFIRMATIONS

Jeremiah 29:11: "For I know the plans I have for you," declares the Lord.
Why it resonates: When everything feels uncertain, the verse whispers that chaos isn't the end of the story. There's a divine blueprint, even if you can't see it yet.

Psalms 34:18: The Lord is near to the brokenhearted and saves the crushed in spirit.
Why it resonates: It reminds me that my pain doesn't push God away—it draws Him closer. You are not abandoned in your pain.

Isaiah 40:31: "But those who hope in the Lord will renew their strength. They will soar on wings like eagles."
Why it resonates: When you're exhausted, this verse offers a vision of rising again—not just surviving but soaring.

Psalms 28:7: "The Lord is my strength and my shield; my heart trusts in him, and he helps me."
Why it resonates: It's a reminder that you don't have to be strong all the time. You're allowed to lean on something greater.

Isaiah 43:2: "When you pass through the waters, I will be with you; they will not sweep over you."
Why it resonates: It doesn't promise a life without storms, but it promises you won't drown in them.

FAITH AND AFFIRMATIONS

John 1:5: "The light shines in the darkness, and the darkness has not overcome it."
Why it resonates: Even the smallest flicker of hope is more powerful than the deepest shadow. Light always wins.

Psalms 46:10: "Be still, and know that I am God."
Why it resonates: In a world that demands constant motion, this verse invites you to pause and find peace in surrender.

Leonard Cohen: "There is a crack in everything; that's how the light gets in."
Why it resonates: Your brokenness isn't a flaw—it's an opening. Healing doesn't mean erasing the cracks but letting them glow.

Khalil Gibran: "Out of suffering have emerged the strongest souls; the most massive characters are seared with scars."
Why it resonates: This quote reframes pain as a forge, not a failure. Your scars are proof of survival, not shame.

Psalm 30:5: "Weeping may last for the night, but joy comes in the morning."
Why it resonates: It's a promise that sorrow is not forever. Morning always comes. And with it, Joy.

MY GO-TO AFFIRMATIONS

I was made for more than fear; no weapon that forms against me shall prosper.

I choose faith over fear. God goes before me. Peace walks with me.

I am safe, I am love, I am free.

I believe in a love that's bigger than anything we can name. When I'm hurting, it helps to remember I am not alone.

I may not see the whole path, but I trust the journey. Even when life feels random, there may still be a loving order—seen or unseen—that is gently guiding me forward.

If a survivor has five minutes and no privacy, what quick grounding practice, breathing, scripture, or mantra can I teach them?

"BREATHE + ANCHOR" PRACTICE
(5 MINUTES, NO PRIVACY NEEDED)

Step 1: Breath of Peace (1 minute)

Inhale slowly through the nose for 4 counts.
Hold for 2 counts.
Exhale gently through the mouth for 6 counts.
Repeat silently for 3-5 rounds.
This slows the nervous system and signals safety to the body.

Step 2: Scripture Whisper (2 minutes)

Choose one short verse that can be repeated silently with
each breath. Here are a few that work beautifully:

"Be still and know" (Psalms 46:10)

"I will not fear" (Isaiah 41:10)

"You are with me" (Psalms 23:4)

"Peace, be still" (Mark 4:39)

Pair the inhale with the first half and the exhale with the
second. For example: Inhale: "Be still" Exhale: "and know"

Step 3: Grounding Mantra (2 minutes)

A quiet, internal mantra to repeat like a heartbeat:
"I am safe, I am here, I am held."

"This moment is mine, I choose Peace."

"God is near, I am not alone."

You can place a hand on your chest or thigh if it feels safe—
just enough to remind the body: I am still here. This practice
is portable, private, and powerful. It does not require a mat, a
room, or even a spoken word—just a breath, presence, and a
whisper of truth.

FINAL ENCOURAGEMENT

Chapter Benediction

May the God who sees you, hold you. May His peace guard your heart and mind like a gentle shield (Philippians 4:7). And may His goodness follow you—even here, even now—into the days ahead.

My deepest hope for everyone who picks up this book is that these words remind them of their sacredness, that even the torn pages of their story are worth reading aloud. That they are not alone and never have been. Whatever comes next, may love meet them there first, and may they never forget that they are the Miracle that they are waiting for.

Final Prayer

God of the universe, God of grace and mercy, Thank you for walking with the one who made it this far. Wrap them now in peace that lingers, in grace that doesn't rush healing. Let the truths planted in these pages bear fruit in quiet moments. Remind them that they are not too broken, not too late, not too lost. May your love be their shelter, and your hope their rising light. And may they never forget—they are deeply known and wholly loved by you.

Amen.

FINAL QUICK TIPS FOR CAYMAN-BASED READERS

All numbers below are confidential & free (calls from FLOW/LIME landlines are toll-free; Digicel mobiles use regular minutes).

If speaking aloud feels unsafe: E-mail CICC (info@cicc.ky) using a private account or the library computer.

Send a WhatsApp voice/text to the Mental Health Helpline (547-6463) or TAYA Lounge (922-2292). Messages auto-delete after 24 hours unless you save them.

Need shelter tonight? Call the CICC hotline; staff will arrange discreet transport day or night.

Outside Cayman but still in crisis? You can live-chat at TheHotline.org or RAINN.org, or text HOME to 741741 for the Crisis Text Line (they'll look up services in your country).

Medical attention after assault: Ask the hospital triage nurse for the on-call CICC advocate; you will not be charged for forensic examination or emergency contraception.

Worried about immigration status? CICC and FRC do not share information with Immigration; help is offered regardless of nationality or visa.

ACKNOWLEDGMENTS

As I reflect on the pages of this book and the path that led me here, I am reminded that no journey is ever walked alone. I owe a deep and abiding gratitude to those who have stood beside me, lifted me, and inspired me along the way.

To my **family**—your constant love, support, and faith have given me the foundation for every dream; you are both my anchor and my compass.

To my **family in Christ**, thank you for being a source of spiritual strength and upliftment. Your prayers, fellowship, and faith have carried me through periods of growth and grace.

To my **past and present work colleagues**, your collaboration, mentorship, and camaraderie have shaped me professionally and personally. I am grateful for the lessons learned, the challenges shared, and the victories celebrated together.

And to **every person who has touched my life in a positive way**, whether through a kind word, a helping hand, or a moment of inspiration, thank you. Your impact may have seemed small, but it was profound.

This book is not just a reflection of my story; it is a tribute to yours as well.

Sharon Yee Spencer

ABOUT THE AUTHOR

Sharon Spencer is a Christian, wife, mother, grandmother, insurance advisor, and cook whose life is a testament to faith, survival, and resilience. Born in Jamaica in 1962, Sharon endured a childhood marked by abandonment, neglect, and abuse. For decades she carried the weight of silence, but in her sixties, she embraced her voice and fulfilled a lifelong dream of becoming an author.

In this courageous debut, *Nobody's Child*, Sharon shares the painful events of her past alongside original poetry and uplifting Bible verses. Her story is one of survival, faith, and healing—a journey from trauma to truth. With raw honesty and spiritual strength, she offers readers a reminder that even the deepest wounds can be touched by God's love.

Now, in the best years of her life, Sharon is living proof that age is just a number and that God can transform brokenness into beauty at any stage. Through every page, she invites readers to reclaim their worth, embrace their faith, and remember that no one is truly nobody's child.

NOTES

www.ingramcontent.com/pod-product-compliance
Lightning Source LLC
Chambersburg PA
CBHW051235120626
46547CB00013B/1658